Swansea

The time of our lives

by David Roberts

**First published in Great Britain in 2018
by Bryngold Books Ltd.
100 Brynau Wood, Cimla,
Neath, South Wales SA11 3YQ.**

**Typesetting, layout,
editing and design
by Bryngold Books**

ISBN: 978-1-905900-50-3

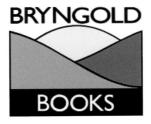

Printed in Wales

www.bryngoldbooks.com

Dedication

Swansea — Time of our lives is dedicated to my wife Cheryl, without whose endless patience, assistance and encouragement neither this book, nor any of those that have gone before would ever have appeared. I really couldn't have done it without her.

About the author

It was an amazing 21 years ago that David Roberts, as a journalist with the South Wales Evening Post, was tasked, with producing a book taking a pictorial look back at Swansea, as it bravely ventured into a new Millennium.

David Roberts

Little could he have realised that the success of Images of Swansea, that first book, would see him continue to produce a similar one for each of the consecutive years in the following two decades and now already entering the third.

Now, the publication of **Swansea — The time of our lives,** brings to a total of 21, his personal tally of titles that take the city's citizens of today on an incredible trip back in time. No other location can lay claim to such a community photographic album with such longevity in its pedigree. The series has been saluted as an incomparable look-back in time which captures the flavour and the feeling of the way the city once was. People, places and events all feature throughout this book's pages along with many more glimpses of the way the city once was.

The pages of **Swansea — The time of our lives,** provide a home for images that will revive many memories for all those who turn its pages. Those same images will endure for long into the future and help tell the story that is Swansea.

Telling the city story

Look at a timeline of Swansea and you will quickly notice that right from its earliest days as a settlement it never appears to have stood still. Some would have it that there has always been something going on. That's putting it simply, but look closely at the history books and you will see that it is also very true.

Down through the centuries, right up to the present day there has indeed always been 'something going on'. Not surprisingly many of the activities covered by this umbrella expression focussed on the River Tawe and the sea beyond. The coming of the Industrial Revolution saw tremendous growth in the city and its hinterland partly because of this and as the name Swansea was stamped on the world so its population grew at speed.

At the beginning of the 19th Century it was teetering on 7,000 persons; just 40 years later that figure had more than doubled to 16,000. So fast was the growth that by the turn of the 20th Century Swansea could boast a populace of 134,000. Today that figure is around 241,000. These are impressive figures and with them came parks, libraries and hospitals. A new guildhall, art gallery and council houses followed. A leisure centre, major shopping complexes and other fine buildings came as the years rolled on. Docklands were turned into a marina, the SA1 business and latterly education district and still the changes come.

All change brings with it controversy and disagreement, but still it happens. The tidal barrage scheme is a prime current example, but huge amounts of money have headed Swansea's way in recent times and the developments they bring will ensure that the city moves with the times. And that, more than anything else, places a value on the images in this book that cannot be underestimated.

The photographs on the following pages show places and events, but more importantly they show too, the faces of some of the people who made this proud city what it is today. Swansea may be Wales' second city, but it is also Wales's best seaside city, one striving to offer the best in higher education and research facilities and a city of which those same 241,000-plus inhabitants can be justifiably proud.

Swansea — The time of our lives and the predecessor, companion titles, combine to tell the story almost up to the present day. Its publication marks something of a coming of age — this is the 21st edition in the same number of years — of a book like no other in Britain. There is none like it that has endured and moved forward with the location it has served. It is a unique project to have become involved in all those years ago, it is also one that could not possibly have endured without the support of a great many residents of the place it reflects, wherever they live, be it near or far from their roots.

A big thank you

Swansea — Time of our lives, is a book which we hope will once again bring much enjoyment to a great many people far and wide. It is the result of photographic contributions, large and small which capture some unique times from the city's past and allow it to be seen from a different perspective, often through the eyes of those who were there, camera in hand. The book's pictures are often not perfect compositions, nor the work of professionals. They are instead, the earthy efforts of ordinary happy snappers whose pictures tell it as it was and are often gems in their own right.

The appearance of **Swansea — Time of our lives,** the 21st book in the series in as many consecutive years would not have been possible without the support of Derek Gabriel, Roy Kneath, Terry Giltinan, David & Gay Mitchell, Raymond & Dorothy Lewis, John Jones, Barry Griffiths, Margaret Childs, Bernard Humphries, Dennis Scanes, Steve Davies, John Southard, Geoff Rees, JV Hughes, Christine Rix, Bill Morris, Hugh Rees, Adeline Evans, Richard and Anne Evans, Bryn Evans, Vivian G Davies, Eric Hill, Graham Davies, Kathryn Owens, Michael Hallet, Stephen Miles, Roy Morgan, Roger Evans, Peter Bailey, David Williams, Brendan Somerville, Des & Diana Jones, David Webborn, Allan Penhorwood, John & Jo Coode, Julie Jones, Roy Payne, Colin & Eileen Payne, Roger Hayman, Susan Reynish, Mrs R Cummings, Dennis Watts, TB Harris, John Griffiths, Hywel Thomas, Godfrey Jones, Philip Chatfield, GJ John, HJ Morgan, Keith & Elizabeth Johnston.

Others without whose involvement **Swansea — Time of our lives,** would not have appeared include David Beynon,d Gerald Gabb, Neil Melbourne and Charlie Wise. And finally, as they say, I must thank my wife Cheryl, without whose support, **Swansea — Time of our lives,** would have been a far poorer publication.

David Roberts

Share your pictures

If you have photographs of people, places or events in and around Swansea right up to recent times then you could play a part in the next Swansea nostalgia book. Simply telephone 01639 643961 or email david.roberts@bryngoldbooks.com to discover the ways in which you can do this. All photographs, transparencies, negatives, black and white or colour, of people, places, events, streets, buildings, schooldays and sport are considered whatever their age or subject. They are all promptly returned. We can also receive your pictures electronically. Meanwhile, if you have missed any of the previous 20 books why not contact us now as some titles are still available to help complete your collection. You can also check out our many other similar titles at:

www.bryngoldbooks.com

An unusual perspective on a vessel receiving attention at Swansea Dry Dock in 1999. Dwarfing all around, it is the Trinity House Vessel, Mermaid.

Pupils of Mayhill Junior school take advantage of a sunny summer's day for a reading lesson in the garden outside their classroom, while their teacher looks on, 1950s. Three of the pupils appear to be reading passages from the book in turn, while the others follow attentitivley.

Members of the Spridgeon family. Among them a Mr Spridgeon who was one of the first LMS station masters at Swansea Victoria station. He is seated on the left alongside his wife. The station opened in 1850 and this photograph was probably taken in the early 1900s.

A shopper at Swansea market watches carefully as a seafood stallholder weighs out a quantity of cockles, late 1960s.

The exterior of the parcel depot at High Street railway station, mid-1980s.

A group of youngsters from Mumbles soak up the atmosphere at the Heineken music festival held in Singleton Park, August 8, 1993.

A South Wales Transport Leyland Olympian double decker, one of seven delivered as its final batch of new double deck vehicles in 1985, seen leaving the Quadrant bus station towards the end of the decade. The former Singleton Street bus station is visible to the right, yet to be converted into a Wilkinson's retail store.

Early construction work underway on the new RNLI lifeboat station alongside Mumbles Pier, February 15, 2013. The previous station can be seen on the left.

Some of the pupils who attended Cila School, Killay, with teacher Mr Davies, 1962.

The new
Mumbles
Lifeboat
inside the
new
Mumbles
Lifeboat
house, 2016.

The Reynish family from Swansea with Noel Edmonds, presenter of the popular TV game show Telly Addicts, of which they were the winners in 1986.

These heads, pictured on April 9, 2014, certainly brought an interesting slant to waiting for a bus at the newly revamped Quadrant bus station. They were among the most popular and intriguing works that were part of Art Across the City in that year. The work was titled The General Public. The four ghostly heads by the Ultimate Holding Company caused quite a stir when they were first installed. They were commissioned as part of the Dylan Thomas 100 celebrations. They were in place for 10 weeks.

Motorcycling enthusiasts who attended the Classic Motorcycle Show organised by Swansea Museum.

The view over Swansea Docks from high up on Kilvey Hill, 2010. Looking down from the same spot today would reveal a far different scene of the area with much redevelopment having taken place in the intervening years.

Youngsters Janice Griffiths and Barbara Thomas in their uniforms for their first day at Glanmor School and Llwyn-y-Bryn School, respectively, mid-1950s.

A group of youngsters from Foxhole Road, on the promenade at Swansea, early 1960s.

Smartly uniformed members of the Womens Junior Air Corps band march along St Helens Road just past its junction with Page Street on Remembrance Day, November 1949.

As they await demolition these properties brought a sad end to a Swansea street that once housed the city offices of a number of insurance companies.

Howard Martin, stands behind Anthony Armstrong Jones, the brother in law of Queen Elizabeth II, while guiding him on a tour of the silk screen department of Swansea College of Art, during a visit to the facility in 1965.

Presentation of floral bouquets to guests
who attended a Christmas Fayre, held at
Toronto Place, physically handicapped
home, Penlan 1970s.

A snowy morning in Uplands didn't stop these hardy
folk from going about their daily business,1980s.

Boarded up properties await demolition on Carmarthen Road, Fforestfach, late 1970s.

Building work underway on the site of the former Pantycelyn Hotel, Oystermouth Road, on July 7, 2015.

Smiles all round as the youngsters of this Swansea family enjoy a sunny, summer's day outing somewhere in Gower, August 1955.

Fishing boats alongside Pilot House wharf, near the entrance to the South Dock basin, mid-1970s.

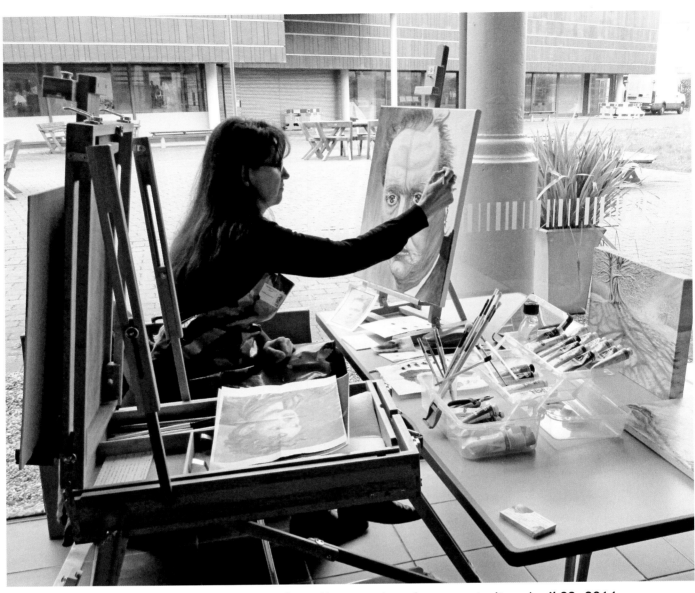

An artist in residence at The National Waterfront Museum at work on a portrait on April 22, 2014.

An ftr metro 'bendy bus' operated by First Cymru heads down The Kingsway during the mid afternoon of June 25, 2015.

Young members of Mayhill Junior School's football squad being awarded a cup for success in a local competition while one of their teachers proudly looks on, 1980s.

Pupils of Powys Avenue Junior School with headmaster, Mr Launchbury, and class teacher Miss Manson, 1964.

Judges, exhibitors and visitors to one of the successful autumn flower shows held at Townhill and Mayhill Community Centre during the 1950s.

Bonymaen Community Centre, 1992.

Batman with one of the employees of the Mettoy toy factory, mid-1970s. The Batmobile was one of its most popular and now most sought after models.

The anti-aircraft gun alongside the River Tawe, and New Cut bridge, 2002. It is a memorial to the air defence of the city during the second world war.

The nothing if not impressive butchery stand of John Mabe at Swansea Market. His white coated staff posing for this picture in the early 1900s could cater for all hotels, hospitals, and public institutions of all kinds.

A terrace of late Georgian buildings in Cambrian Place after refurbishment, 1988. The Assembly Rooms building is on the left.

The Russian cruise ship Leonid Brezhnev at Swansea's King's Dock, 1986.

Staff of Swansea Sound and South Wales Transport stand alongside a bus that was covered with an advertisement for the radio station in the 1980s.

Members of the St Illtyd's women's darts team, Christmas 1990.

Young girls of a class at Mayhill Junior School joined by their teacher, dressed in traditional Welsh costume for their St David's Day celebrations, mid-1950s.

This view up Wind Street from Quay Parade in 1982 offers a much different picture to that of today. Many of the businesses that can be picked out with a keen eye have long vanished from the city retail scene.

Members of the first year cross country team at Olchfa Comprehensive School, with their PE teacher, 1986.

The Swiss chalet viewed through the leafless trees at Singleton Park, on a sunny, late spring afternoon, April, 1966.

The Mermaid Hotel, Southend, January 1993, shortly before its demolition following a fire.

This Swansea Air Cadets band impressed the crowd at the annual fete held at the Ford Motor Company's Jersey Marine plant with both their marching and musical ability, 1976.

Swansea Councillor Chris Thomas plants a tree in the centre of Mayhill School with the help of a pupil. The school has now been renamed Seaview Primary.

Archie, one of the regular drivers of the ambulance that conveyed patients from Singleton hospital to outlying convalescent homes in the city such as Llwynderw and Cwmdonkin. He is pictured with his vehicle outside the entrance of the hospital mid-1970s.

Mayor, Councillor DF Bevan, looks on during the presentation of bouquets to the Lady Mayoress, Mrs Bartlett-Williams and an accompanying guest at a function held at Longfields home, early 1960s.

Swansea's 'Big Six' fire engine wasn't hurrying to the scene of another fire on this occasion, simply proceeding at a leisurely pace among the floats that took part in the Lord Mayor's Parade, 1975.

The occupant of Banc Villa, Cefn Road, Bonymaen, outside her thatched roof home, 1930's.

A group of friends prepare to set off from Sea View Terrace, North Hill for a holiday at Butlins, 1965.

Two football teams stand in silence and in tribute to a former member of one of the clubs who had passed away, late 1950s.

No doubt there would have been many tales told of days long gone when this group of former Sketty Youth Club members got together for a reunion at Sketty Hall.

Work underway on the Mumbles sewer outfall project, mid-1930s. While much can be seen going on above ground, the bottom picture shows a number of men with hand tools, hewing out one of the underground chambers. The project was officially opened in 1937.

WARNING
PASSAGE
PROHIBITED
TO ALL
VESSELS

Players and officials of Langland
Rugby Club, 1924-5 season.

Some of the students at Swansea Secondary Technical School for girls 1959-1960.

Some of the guests and officials who attended the official opening of Dunvant Rugby Club. The cake being cut would surely have been impressive, but sadly was left out of this shot!

Oxford Street shoppers turn to look at a group of usherettes from the Maxime cinema, Sketty, posing for the camera with umbrellas, late 1940s. The Maxime opened in 1932 and became The Odeon, Sketty in 1947.

Bus drivers Tony Smith and Allan Penhorwood who won the Morriston Hospital doubles tournament in 1981. They played for the Magnet Club darts team which was the local club of South Wales Transport.

William Jenkins and his children outside St Thomas Church 1939.

Looking across flattened Temple Street towards Castle Street during clearance work after the bombing that took place in the Second World War.

Swansea University Chemistry Department technicians, 1962.

Nearing the end, the former British Home Stores outlet in Princess Way advertises its terms for savvy shoppers shortly before it closed its doors for the last time, April 27, 2016.

Usherettes at the Albert Hall cinema gather for one last picture together on their last night on duty before its closure. It later went on to operate as a bingo hall, but that too closed in 2007.

Paddling at Three Cliffs Bay, Gower with attire that might be unusual for such an event today, but this early 1950s family seemed to enjoy the experience nonetheless.

Looking across the roundabout at the top of The Kingsway, 1971. The roundabout was later excavated to create a pedestrian underpass only to be filled in again to accommodate 21st Century traffic flow changes.

A young man stands and looks over the River Tawe and the many industrial locations along its banks from an eastside vantage point, late 1950s.

Mr Greening with one of his first motor lorries outside his home in Gower Road, Upper Killay, early 1950s.

The wreck of the pleasure vessel Prince Ivanhoe aground at Port Eynon, Gower. The vessel was beached there on August 3, 1981 after hitting an underwater obstruction while carrying a full complement of passengers. She was eventually dismantled on the spot. Work to do this had already begun when this picture was taken. FAR LEFT: Onlookers view the sad hulk from the shoreline.

Captain Arthur Harris receiving the Swansea Football League Division One Championship trophy on behalf of the Tower United team from league president Abe Freedman, 1962-63 season.

The cast of the pantomime Cinderella, performed at the Welcome Inn, Mynyddbach Common over two days to raise funds for Ty Hafan children's hospice in February 2001. The performances raised more than £750.

A teacher inspects the results of the efforts of these boys after a basket weaving class at Mayhill Junior School, mid-1950s.

Members and officials of Swansea Police Rugby Club, 1966/67 season.

Pupils of Mayhill Junior School show off the magnificent display of produce they had gathered for their annual Harvest Festival, topped off by a sheaf of bread, mid-1950s.

General cargo vessels berthed at King's Dock, mid-1960s.

Afternoon shoppers in Oxford Street on August 8, 2002.

The fish and chip shop owned by Mrs. F Hawkes at the junction of Dyfatty Street and Tontine Street. Her son Edward is seen in its doorway with the family dog shortly before the outbreak of the Second World War.

A signalman at work in his Gorseinon signal box, late 1950s.

The entrance hall and stairway at the building constructed to house the offices of West Glamorgan County Council and latterly Swansea City Council's civic centre, September 10, 2015.

Looking under one of the city's few remaining former railway arches across busy Oystermouth Road towards the Tesco Marina store, 2004.

Looking towards Castle Gardens from its junction with Upper and Lower Union Street, 1970s.

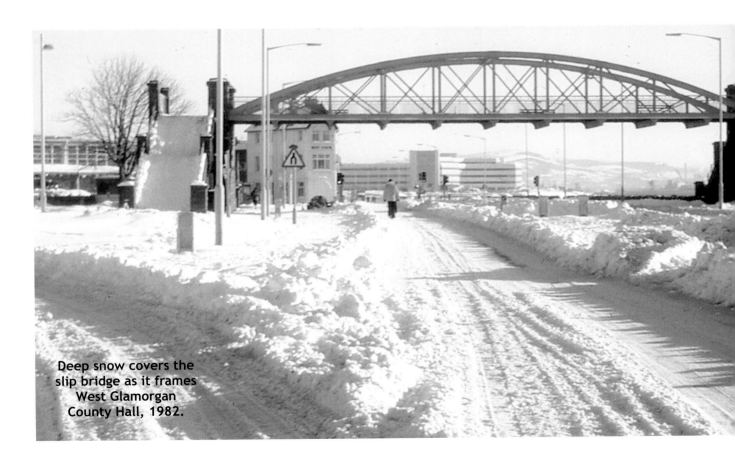

Deep snow covers the slip bridge as it frames West Glamorgan County Hall, 1982.

Staff of the Briggs tyre depot, 1966.

Waiting for their signal at High Street station are the driver and fireman of 4-6-0 Castle Class steam locomotive, Earl of Shaftsbury.

A panorama of the South Dock and behind, a Swansea far different
to that which exists today, captured in the mid-1960s.

Young girls dressed in traditional Welsh costume, to celebrate St David's Day at Mount Pleasant, mid-1970s.

There were few takers for some skiing experience when this picture of the once popular artificial ski slope at Morfa was taken in 2000.

A Peckett steam locomotive hauls two carriages of passengers along about two miles of track preserved by the Swansea Vale Railway Society between Upper Bank, Pentrechwyth and Six Pit Junction, Llansamlet. The trip was a popular bank holiday attraction until vandalism defeated society members in 2008.

The bridge over the River Tawe that was once the main eastern gateway to the city for road traffic, 1955.

Pre-demolition images of the famous Vetch Field ground that held so many memories, both good and bad, for long time, dyed in the wool Swansea City supporters.

A rare peep inside the projection room of the Albert Hall cinema with one of its projectionists ready to run the latest blockbuster film.

Construction work underway near Pockett's Wharf, Swansea Marina, mid-1980s.

The goods shed at High Street railway station, 1980s.

Swansea Imperial Singers prepare to perform at a Christmas event, 1947. Their accompanist at the piano was Olive Annie Rees.

Shoppers in Oxford Street on a November day mid-1980s.

The conductor of a South Wales Transport double decker waits alongside St Mary's Church, before heading off on his next run to Margam, late 1960s.

Two gas storage Hortonspheres at BP Oils Queen's Dock terminal, early 1980s.

A smartly dressed Alwyn Howells, a familiar figure at Cefn Road, Bonymaen, 1930s.

Brother and sister Emrys and Doris John, with the Swansea Vale Spelter Works in the background, 1929.

The Helwick lightship and Picton Sea Eagle floating restaurant, tower over other smaller craft in the South Dock marina, late 1980s.

A group of regulars outside the Brynmelin public house, Christmas Day, 1980.

Railway sidings near Victoria station crammed with coal and mineral wagons, late 1920s.

Looking across the junction of High Street and Alexandra Road, from Ivey Place, 1985.

Hill Chapel Sunday School members with their teachers take time out from an outing to pose for the camera.

Swansea's former Guildhall, Somerset Place, 1988.

The Mumbles Train at Blackpill, early 1950s. The overhead bridge carried the railway line from Victoria station out of the city.

Looking across a flower-filled Castle Gardens, towards Swansea Castle then occupied by the South Wales Evening Post, mid-1950s.

This tank locomotive is crossing Oystermouth Road, near what today is its junction with West Way. It was on the low-level line that linked the South Dock with Swansea gasworks, August 1924.

Engineering department employees at the Ravenhill depot of South Wales Transport, 1970.

The car ferry MV Superferry arriving at King's Dock, in March 1993 before beginning the regular car ferry link between Swansea and Cork in Ireland.

Prince Edward seen engaging with pupils during a visit to Olchfa School, Sketty, 1992.

A crane hoists huge carved gable stones into place on the pine end of a development of new self contained flats at Somerset Place, late 1987.

Two members of the crew of a Swansea fishing vessel off The Smalls Lighthouse.

Restored steam locomotive King George V leaves Swansea via the Hafod loop and heading westwards with an enthusiasts' special titled The Carmarthen Express, 1987. As the first of the class, locomotive No. 6000 was specifically named after the then monarch of the United Kingdom, King George V. Early in its life, the locomotive was shipped to the United States in August 1927 to feature in the B&O's centenary celebrations. During the celebrations it was presented with a bell and a plaque, and these are carried to this day.

Crowds throng the stands and tents at Pontardawe Folk Festival, 1976.

Looking across the city centre towards St Mary's Church from building construction, mid-1970s.

Family and friends surround city bride Eileen Gough and her groom Leslie Mees at the reception which followed their wedding in the early 1950s.

Spit and sawdust was the order of the day in the 1950s when these two mates, deep in conversation, met in their favourite drinking haunt, the Lord Nelson public house, in High Street.

Participants in the Lord Mayor's Parade pass St Helen's rugby and cricket ground as they head along Oystermouth Road,1975.

The former Alexandra Towing Company tug, Alfred after finishing its duties at Swansea Docks, 1988.

Looking from Milton Terrace along Watkin Street, Mount Pleasant after a heavy snowfall, November 2005.

A mixed goods train waits to proceed through Swansea Bay station while traffic on the road alongside slips and slithers after an overnight snowfall, 1963.

Swansea RFC captained by Stuart Davies prepare to meet the 6th Springboks in 1969.

The mud-caked hulk of the copper ore boat Lady Quirk, left rotting on a mudbank near New Cut bridge on the River Tawe at low tide, late 1980s.

Gravestones for dogs at Clyne Park, August 2004.

A Mumbles tram car waits at the pier terminus before heading back into Swansea, early 1930s.

Members of Gors School cricket team in 1968 with their teacher and headteacher. Captain, Stephen Gough, is in the front row, second from the right.

Traffic at the busy Morriston Cross intersection, 2006.

Dave Stephens, mill manager at the Maritime & Industrial Museum, working the loom of the former Neath Abbey woollen mill which was housed at the museum, mid-1980s.

A policewoman stands on point duty at the pedestrian crossing near the College Street junction with Kingsway roundabout before the construction of a multi-directional subway, late 1960s.

Regulars of the Cardiff Arms public house, which stood at the junction of King's Lane and The Strand, enjoy a pint of their favourite ale and a good natter no doubt, 1972.

The Queen Mother at the service of reconsecration and re-opening of St Mary's Church after a long wait to rebuild it following bomb damage inflicted in the Second World War, May 28, 1959.

Looking across to the iconic Weaver's Flour Mill buildings from Wind Street, early 1970s. Built in 1898, it was the earliest reinforced concrete building in Wales.

Striding smartly along Castle Street this city jazz band was part of a parade in the 1970s.

The colourfully decorated wall of the Dylan Thomas Theatre, Gloucester Place, early 1990s.

Demolition of Oxford Street School looking towards shops and restaurants in Oxford Street.

Lord Mayor Susan Jones with Anne Aston, hostess of TV's Golden Shot fame on a visit to the city, 1978.

Some of the policemen who kept law and order around Swansea Docks.

Beach front properties cling to the promenade at Swansea maritime quarter, mid-1990s.

A class of pupils at Powys Avenue Junior School with their teacher Miss Trollope, 1968.

The former Lars Knutsen shipping chandlery in The Strand, 1987. This building is now occupied by the Walkabout bar.

Looking along Somerset Place towards Quay Parade and Wind Street, late 1960s. The former Swansea Guildhall is on the right.

A team of Freightliner drivers at their depot in Crymlyn Burrows, 1970.

Pupils of first year classes at Gendros Junior School on a visit to Singleton Park, autumn 1971.

Construction work underway on the New Cut road bridge over the River Tawe early 1970s.

Prefab homes at Foresthall, Fforestfach, mid-1950s.

It's eyes down for a special bingo session at Mecca Bingo to raise money for heart research.

Swansea City Councillor Susan Jones is installed as Lord Mayor, May 1978.

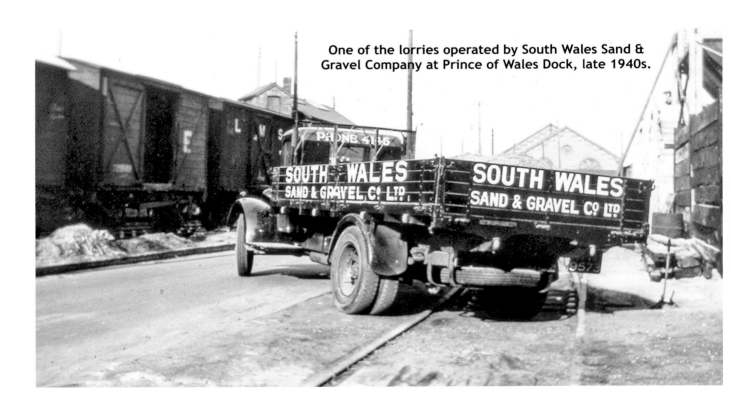

One of the lorries operated by South Wales Sand &
Gravel Company at Prince of Wales Dock, late 1940s.

Flooding at Sandfields after heavy
rainfall,1972. BELOW: The result
of a similar event in Spring Terrace and
Argyle Street, early 1960s.

Looking down on New Cut bridge, the St Thomas railway bridge and the railway bridge that crossed Fabian Way into the docks, February 28, 1985. The Norwegian Church now stands on a new, nearby site in SA1.

This group of smoking stacks towered over the Grovesend steelworks, Gorseinon, early 1900s.

The Trinity House vessel Patricia berthed at King's Dock, 1998.

A United Welsh double decker turns into the Kingsway from Christina Street, mid-1950s. This Bristol-make vehicle served the company from June 1952 until it was converted into a breakdown vehicle in February 1965.

Chicago rock cafe, St Mary Street on August 28, 2003. This popular restaurant bar operated for many years. The location is now occupied by Hogarth's gin bar.

Pupils of Class 1C at Dunvant Primary School with their teacher Mrs J Childs, early 1970s.

Horses and carts outside Bullins Stables at Heathfield Street, early 1920s. Mount Pleasant Chapel is behind.

A group of participants help to pull one of the competing boats out of the water after a successful 1972 Mumbles yachting regatta.

BBC Wales TV presenter Vincent Kane recording a current affairs programme with a Swansea backdrop, early 1970s. The view looking up the lower Swansea valley shows that reclamation work had yet to get seriously underway on what was acknowledged as an industrial wasteland.

A youngster sits at a family grave alongside Morriston Crematorium, August, 1961.

Members of the football team run at The Magnet Club, the staff club of the South Wales Transport Company at its Ravenhill depot, early 1970s.

Rebuilding work underway on St Mary's Church, 1957.

A service of dedication of the stained glass window commemorating the 1947 Mumbles Lifeboat disaster crew, at All Saint's Church, Mumbles.

Pupils of Mayhill School who took part in its Nativity play, Christmas 1982.

A High Street thronged with people viewed from Castle Street, 1930s.

The Mumbles train at Rutland Street, opposite its depot, late 1950s.

The presentation of trophies to successful entrants in an art competition sponsored by Alcoa for Swansea Schools, 1977.

The ticket desk and confectionery counter in the foyer of the Albert Hall cinema.

A fitter prepares to renew the tyres on one of the South Wales Transport Company's buses, late 1950s.

High Street railway station after heavy snowfall, 1980s.

A visit to Mumbles was never complete without a visit to the Big Apple which offered everything you could need for a day on the sands.

Locomotives and wagons at the coal stage at Landore locomotive depot, mid-1950s.

Participants in a pageant at Mayhill School, early 1960s.

An open air meeting of High Street Salvation Army Corps band alongside High Street railway station, mid-1960s.

Some of those who took part in one of the successful Gang Shows staged by Scouts, Cubs, Guides and Brownies during the 1970s.

Repair work underway on one of the piers at Swansea Docks, early 1960s.

Richard Branson's Virgin Atlantic Challenger II attracts attention on the quayside at Swansea Marina after the 72ft vessel smashed the world record for the fastest ever crossing of the Atlantic. Sir Richard shaved two hours off the existing record with his time of three days, eight hours and 31 minutes.

Participants aboard a float depicting the musical Wizard of Oz, one of the many colourful spectacles that made up the Eastside carnival parade, 1993.

The Orange House, a one time popular bar, 2003. It occupied the site of what was formerly Tesco's Kingsway store when that relocated to Oystermouth Road.

Just some of the many ways that the residents of Llanddewi, Gower, celebrated the Coronation of Queen Elizabeth II, in June 1953. The events centred on a barn at a farm in Cheriton and featured a fancy dress parade, a tea party and best of all was the provision of a TV on which they could watch the events of the day. For many it was the first time they had ever seen a TV!

One of the Scout troops which took part in a 1980s carnival.

Fishermen at the end of Mumbles Pier, August, 1964.

Women of Sandfields who were the cleaning staff of Swansea Guildhall on the occasion of the retirement of their manager.

The Oscar Chess car showroom and garage in Gloucester Place, early 1959. This is now the site of the Dylan Thomas Theatre.

Traffic on Victoria Road with the forecourt of Victoria railway station just visible behind the wall on the left. York Place English Baptist Chapel is on the right, early 1960s.

Traffic and pedestrians at the junction of High Street, Castle Street, College Street and Welcome Lane, early 1960s.

Swansea captain Harry Griffiths and Burnley captain Jim Adamson shake hands before the referee tosses a coin at the start of the 1962 Cup replay match between the two teams at Vetch Field.

120

Swansea Bay railway station, mid-1950s.
Wind blown sand, was a near permanent
problem here and along the rest of this
seafront line, particularly during the winter.

Drivers and conductors of the Mumbles
Railway after finishing their final shifts
on the day it closed in January, 1960.

A 1930s carnival procession makes its way along Walter Road, much to the delight of the watching crowds which lined the pavement.

A summertime view across picturesque Castle Gardens looking towards the mock Tudor facade of buildings on the east side of Caer Street, early 1960s. Now Castle Square, the buildings remain, but the oasis that was the gardens has long since vanished and is much lamented by many.

A single deck tramcar alongside the Commercial Inn at the junction of Llangyfelach Road and Eaton Road, early 1900s.

The South Wales Transport bus company's garage in Brunswick Street, prior to rebuilding, late 1960s.

A group of late 1930s motorcycle enthusiasts.

Looking along Singleton Street, towards
Western Street, late 1960s.

The giant arched steel skeleton that formed the support for the main glass roof of Swansea market under construction, late 1950s. BELOW: An interior view of the roof which to this day provides cover for the market's many stalls and countless shoppers it serves throughout the week.

Plymouth Street looking across acres of parking made possible by the wartime bombing
of Swansea, mid-1970s. Jeffreys Motors is on the left. Oldway house is in the background.
The site of the two gas holders is now occupied by Tesco's Marina store.

The impressive, landmark clock tower of the Guildhall, mid-1950s.

Sculptor Philip Chatfield at his workshop in Pier Street. Pictured here are some of the fascinating sculptures, at various stages of their creation, that he produced on commission for erection around the Maritime Quarter, during the 1980s.

Headteacher Mr Ken Bailey and members of staff at Oystermouth Junior Comprehensive School, autumn term 1979.

Oxford Street looking eastwards towards Temple Street, early 1900s.

Mr Bert Arnold conducting Swansea Citadel Salvation Army Band when they played outside his house in Spring Terrace on the occasion of his 80th birthday. Bert had formerly been its bandmaster, late 1970s.

A giant snowman on the green near the Guildhall during heavy snow, 1963.

The swing bridge that carried traffic over the channel linking the South Dock and South Dock basin near the pump house before the creation of the marina. In the background is the Coastlines warehouse that became Swansea Industrial and Maritime museum, latterly the site of the National Waterfront museum.

Work underway on the creation of the Quay Parade underpass leading from Adelaide Street to Wind Street. The underpass was opened in 1966.

Paddling at Three Cliffs Bay, Gower. Not perhaps the best attire for the task, but enjoyable just the same for these two ladies!

Traffic travels along Victoria Road after the removal of the high level railway bridge that crossed the road alongside Swansea Museum, late 1960s. On the top right can be seen the former Unifloc building and that of the Powell Duffryn mining company. Both buildings have since been demolished.

Girls of Llwyn-y-Bryn School, at High Street railway station, March 1964, on their way to Venice to board the MS Dunera for an educational cruise around the Mediterranean.

The South Dock basin being filled in, late 1960s. When this work was complete it was eventually re-excavated and is today a modern marina. The tall building in the centre background is the current Pump House restaurant and pub.

Early construction work on West Glamorgan County Hall, now Swansea Civic Centre. The properties alongside were later demolished. early 1980s.

The corner of Alexandra Road and High Street opposite the railway station. The Grand Hotel is on the left, mid-1950s.

Swansea City players including John Toshack aboard the open top double decker bus that carried them on a victory parade through the city centre to celebrate the club winning promotion to Division One, 1981.

Looking over the city from Mount Pleasant, early 1950s. The Plaza cinema can be seen in the centre background.

Houses in lower Horton, Gower, early 1920s.

Senior citizens who were regulars at the Townhill and Mayhill centre in happy mood as they prepare to set off for an outing, 1960.

Looking along Oystermouth Road towards Swansea prison, with barely a vehicle in sight, mid-1960s.

The back of the former Palace Theatre, a picture that could not be replicated today as the area surrounding it has given way to a mixture of housing.

The proprietor of a Rent-a-Bike business based at Mumbles for a number of summer seasons, waits for his next customer, 1990s.

An AEC Bridgemaster double decker emerges from the still under construction new office and garage of the South Wales Transport bus company's depot in Brunswick Street, 1970.

A steam hauled train passes the signal box at Cockett railway station, mid-1950s.

Swansea soprano, Grace Thomas, later Gough, auditioning for impresario Lee Lawrence in the Empire Theatre, Oxford Street. Grace later joined the chorus of the Welsh National Opera.

This group of sailor girls complete with their bearded captain were taking part in a 1980s city carnival.

Members of Ragged School AFC celebrate after their West Wales FA cup win at the Vetch Field, April 1993.

Morfa Bridge, a Grade II listed building in Landore, was built in 1909 to link the Morfa and Upper Bank works by rail. This picture taken in the early 1980s shows Morfa Athletic Stadium to the right. This has been replaced by a B&Q store.

A number of steam locomotives await their turn of duty at Landore depot, early 1950s.

Singleton Hospital, with some of the rooftops
of Derwen Fawr in the background, mid-1970s.

Members, officials and guests at
the annual presentation dinner
of Fforestfach AFC, 1952.

The Swansea Pilot Cutter Benson, pulls alongside the MV Balmoral to put a pilot aboard for her journey into the mouth of the River Tawe.

Somerset place and former Swansea Harbour Trust office with its clock tower. This building is now Morgan's Hotel. On the right is Coleridge House.

Looking up the River Tawe towards the Penlan skyline, mid 1980s. Jeffreys Court tower block stands visible on the left and the water tower in Heol Cadifor on the right.

Two young girls bring a touch of the Dutch bulb fields to a 1980s city parade.

The Swansea — Cork ferry vessel Superferry, at Swansea Ferryport, late 1990s.

Looking over the back gardens of Princess Street, early 1950s.

Guides struggle to hold their flag despite inclement weather conditions when they, together with colleagues from across West Glamorgan, were inspected by Lady Baden Powell at Singleton Park, 1982.

Cars parked on the site of what is now the Quadrant Shopping Centre, late 1960s.

The ruins of St Mary's Church before work began on its restoration after wartime bomb damage. Alongside, a view of the interior after rebuilding.

Workmen and machinery inside Hafod Copper Works, early 1900s.

The decaying remains of some of the offices of Hafod Copper Works, mid-1980s.

Elim Church stands watch over construction work at Alexandra Road, 1980s.

Pupils take part in a 'Theatre in Education' project on American settlement, at Mayhill Junior School, 1975.

Nursing staff at Mount Pleasant Hospital during a Christmas carol singing session, late 1970s.

Pupils at Cwm Infants School, Jersey Road, Bonymaen, with their teacher and headteacher, 1977.

One of the amazing creations that greeted judges of a sand sculpting competition on a Gower beach in the late 1990s.

A group of the first HND business studies students at Swansea College of Technology after their final exams, May, 1964.

Shoppers in Oxford Street in the run up to Christmas, late 1980s.

Pupils of Mynddbach Comprehensive School, who took part in the learners under 15 age group choral speaking party competition and won first prize at the Royal National Eistedfodd of Wales when it was held in Port Talbot, 1966.

A bird's eye view of part of Brynhyfryd, early 2000s.

Two cranes tower over early construction work on the original DVLA building at Clase, Morriston, early 1970s.

Players and officials of one of the football teams of Swansea Boys Club, 1950s.

A view over Townhill, 1990s.

Donald Evans, a maths teacher at Pentrehafod Comprehensive School, early 1980s.

The Goose bar and restaurant, Wind Street, before its many name changes, 2002.

Members of St Joseph's military band, 1970s.

One of the many defensive pill boxes built, and still surviving, on the seaward side of Queen's Dock.

First year pupils at Mynddbach, with their Welsh teachers, Miss J Hughes and Miss M Lewis, seen at either end of the front row visited the Urdd Youth Camp at Llangranog, 1958.

A line up of AEC double deckers of different generations inside the South Wales Transport Company's Brunswick Street depot, early 1970s.

Gardening guru Percy Thrower of TV fame on a visit to a gardening project at Gorseinon Hospital, 1976.

The Morfa Regional Athletics Track just after completion in 1981 prior to the erection of the grandstand. B&Q occupies the site now, while the Liberty Stadium was built on the vacant ground above it and across the River Tawe.

The magnificent sailing vessel Alva of Stockholm, Sweden waits to enter the South Dock basin in the 1980s. She was the training ship for the Maritime Institute of Sweden.

The Adelphi public house,
Wind Street, 2003.

The smiling driver of BR locomotive 4035, Harlech Castle, leans out of his cab prior to setting off from High Street railway station, early 1950s. The locomotive was for many years based at Landore depot.

Inside Swansea library in its new home at the Oystermouth Road Civic Centre, July 7, 2015.

Two images of the hi-jinks and hard work that combined to make this Mumbles Raft Race a success both on and offshore.

166

Children of members of the National Fire Service Accommodation Department at the Guildhall for their annual Christmas party, 1943.

Popular comedian Frankie Howard during a performance at the Blue Anchor Hotel, Penclawdd.

Looking across Swansea Bay towards Kilvey Hill from Mumbles, late 1990s.

A dedicated supporter puts his point across at a meeting of Townhill Labour group in the 1960s.

The junction of Singleton Street and Nelson Street, early 1970s.

Many will remember working in pairs, just as these 1950s Swansea junior school children are doing.

The Littlewoods store, opposite St Mary's Church, 1980s. Today it is home to a Primark fashion store.

169

A late 1950s bird's eye view of the centre of Swansea. It shows that much rebuilding had, by this time, taken place after acres of the city were flattened by bombing during the Second World War.

Looking over the city from Mount Pleasant. The lines of cars are on the top floors of The Kingsway multi-storey car park. Behind can be seen the Odeon cinema, mid-1970s.

Swansea women's hockey team, with coach, 1962-3 season.

This wooden figure of eight railway, an early incarnation of today's huge roller coasters, was built near Oystermouth Square, Mumbles. It opened on May 28, 1909 and ran until at least 1918. These may have been some of its first riders. It was later sold and rebuilt at Coney Beach Amusement Park, Porthcawl.

Residents of Gendros Crescent and the surrounding area gather for a photograph during their celebrations to mark VJ Day, August 15, 1945. This was the day at the end of the Second World War when Japan surrendered unconditionally and thereby brought an end to the war.

Gordon Howard and his bride Mary Williams with attendants and guests after their wedding at Calfaria Baptist Chapel, Ravenhill, 1970s.

A visitor rests at the gateway to Oystermouth Castle, late 1970s.

Two views of the David Evans department store that will bring back many memories for those who flocked through its doors in the years when it occupied pole position on the Princess Way retail strip.

Players and officials of Townhill football team proudly display a trophy they won after a successful season in the 1970s.

The pleasure vessel MV Balmoral berths at Swansea Ferryport on a visit to collect passengers, 2017.

Swansea central police station,
Orchard Street, late 1990s.

The Swansea Boys Club team who were finalists in the Umbro Veterans tournament at Wembley Stadium, 1999 pictured with club officials. The teams name can be seen in lights above them.

Looking over the white clad rooftops of the city centre after an overnight snowfall, November 20, 2006.

Single deck tramcar No 78 on its run, outbound from High Street and heading for Cwmbwrla, late 1930s.

South Wales Transport bus company staff including its signwriter and coachbuilders with Truman representatives alongside the AEC Regent V double decker that was painted as a country pub to celebrate Truman's centenary. This was the first time such a project had been undertaken by South Wales Transport.

Brunswick United AFC at a Swansea League Cup match they played at Vetch Field, 1925-26.

Members of the civil engineering team responsible for the construction of Mumbles sewer outfall, early 1930s.

The road linking Limeslade and Mumbles, late 1930s. Mumbles lighthouse can be seen at the top right.

Members of the Girton House Choir at Glanmor School for Girls who were successful in a choral competition at the Royal National Eisteddfod of Wales at Rhyl, 1953.

Tobacconist Alfred Davies had shops in College Street, Oxford Street as well as this one in Castle Street, 1903.

Mumbles Yacht Club, shortly before construction of Verdi's ice cream parlour in front of it, 1993.

Rosyth No 1, the steam locomotive that for many years was homed at the Maritime & Industrial museum on a low loader vehicle outside Swansea Guildhall. It is now currently operational on the Pontypool and Blaenavon Railway.

Created around the hulk of a former fishing trawler to look like a Spanish galleon, the Picton Sea Eagle was towed from Milford Haven to Swansea in July 1987 and for some years operated as a floating restaurant, berthed in the South Dock.

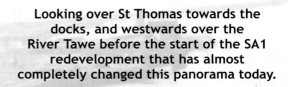

Looking over St Thomas towards the docks, and westwards over the River Tawe before the start of the SA1 redevelopment that has almost completely changed this panorama today.

Looking along Neath Road, Plasmarl, towards Landore, 1976.

Reformed Parc Llewellyn bowls club 1990, Ron Surman, second from the left was the driving force behind the reformation.

Weaver's Flour Mill and the high level Cuba railway bridge dominate Quay Parade, late 1960s.

Drivers and conductors of the Mumbles Railway after finishing their final shifts on the day it closed on January 5, 1960.

The B+I line roll on-roll off car ferry Innisfallen arrives at Swansea Ferryport for the first time. BELOW: The crowd of company officials and civic dignitaries who lined the quayside to welcome the vessel on April 10, 1969. It operated for many years between Swansea and Cork in Ireland.

The former Lewis Lewis department store, High Street, and right, a glass dome is carefully lowered to the ground watched by members of the crew carrying out its eventual demolition. It closed in 1973, but the building had been home to the Bejam frozen food store on the ground floor and the Jobcentre above for a number of years. It had later provided a temporary home to an art gallery and call centre.

Building of the
C&A fashion
store 1972.

Looking up High
Street from Castle
Street, towards
the construction
of Oldway House,
early 1970s.

189

The former Alcoa plant,
Waunarlwydd, 2001.

Carnival kings and queens at a 1980s Eastside carnival.

A very quiet High Street, Gorseinon, early 1920s.

Unloaded from transatlantic supply ships these P47 & P48 fighter aircraft are seen on the dockside at Swansea, September 1944 in the closing years of the Second World War.

Looking across Swansea Bay from Mumbles Hill, early 1970s, before the building of Knab Rock slipway and Verdi's ice cream parlour.

Looking down on Swansea Museum, Victoria Road, from the top of BT tower, February 28, 1985.